PHYLLIS DILLER'S housekeeping hints

PHYLLIS DILLER'S housekeeping hints

Introduction by Bob Hope

Drawings by Susan Perl

DOUBLEDAY AND COMPANY, INC.
GARDEN CITY, NEW YORK

Publishing Consultant: J. P. Tarcher, Inc.

Dedicated to all

the ladies

who would rather

skip

the housework

Introduction

This book is the work of Phyllis Diller, the lady with a thousand gags. One thousand and two . . . I forgot her face and figure.

Phyllis is the only woman (that's just a wild guess) I know who was refused a subscription to *Good Housekeeping*. You'll understand why if you've ever visited her home. I did . . . on the bat's day off.

Have you ever seen her living room? Have you seen the Surveyor moon pictures? You've seen her living room. The rug is so deep in dust the moths carry a pick and shovel. Her refrigerator door has so many fingerprints on it the FBI uses it to train agents.

When it comes to cooking, Phyllis has the Lucrezia Borgia seal of approval. The last time she had a picnic the ants picketed. You've heard about people who can't boil water? Phyllis can . . . she calls it soup. Her kitchen is so poorly organized she keeps a mouse on a leash so she can find the cheese. She shops between the main course and dessert. She has the only dining room table I know with a garbage disposal for a centerpiece. And you can be sure her family always brushes after every meal . . . it's so convenient . . . they're always so close to the toothbrush.

So who's better qualified to write a book on "What's New in Housekeeping?"

BOB HOPE

Foreword

Since there is no Humane Society for Housewives, and since housewives can never say, "My contract expires at midnight and it will not be renewed unless..." I have written a book to help. I can't bear to see women doing a lot of work for nothing.

By clever thinking, housewives may stay away from hard labor and still create the picture of being "the mother in the book." For instance, when you're out in the evening you can make the statement, "I was on my feet for hours tonight getting supper." You don't have to honestly add, "They were short of help at the drive-in and I was at the end of a long line."

This book is filled with such helpful half-truths, quarter-truths, even 1/64 truths. Just like I'm going to say, "This book was recommended by a marriage counselor," and I won't add, "who wanted some business."

PHYLLIS DILLER

Table of Contents

CHAPTER I

How to Get the Chenille Marks off Your Face When the Doorbell Rings

... I Was Trampled by a White Elephant; Remember, That Dirt Belongs to You; Exercise Your Right Not to Exercise; Where There's Smoke, It's Usually Only Dirt; Dishonesty Is the Best Policy; Beauty and the Beast; Meet the Presser; Keep Your Back to Reality

CHAPTER II

What to Say When a Moth Flies Out of the Oven

... The Casualty List Hasn't Been Released Yet; I Was Booked for Inattentive Cooking; Expecting the Unexpected; Marketing Made Easy; Recipes; Is It A Pie? Is It A Cake? It's A Casserole!; What Heloise Doesn't Tell You; A Perfect Waste of Calories; Applied Appliances

CHAPTER I

How To Get
The Chenille Marks Off
Your Face
When The Doorbell Rings

Cleaning your house
While your kids are still growing
Is like shoveling the walk
Before it stops snowing.

THE SLOPPY HOUSEKEEPER'S ALMANAC

I am an immaculate housekeeper. I'm clean, but the house is a mess. I suspected I wouldn't be the perfect housewife the way I botched up the wedding cake.

They won't even sell me *Good Housekeeping* magazine. They're afraid it might be seen in my home. And I can't blame them. I'm such a lousy housekeeper even the white pages in my phone book are yellow.

I know people who are so clean you can eat off their floors. You can't eat off my table. Fang, my husband, says the only thing domestic about me is that I was born in this country.

Some women have qualities that take away the need for being a domestic expert, but unfortunately, I do not. When I stand next to Jayne Mansfield I feel like a cake with the baking powder left out.

And household ability wouldn't matter if I were a financial genius, but if I invested in a mouth wash stock, bad breath would suddenly become popular.

Besides this, I live next door to Mrs. Clean, who bleaches her *snow*. She's got dust cloths for her dust cloths. Everything at her house folds up and puts away. She has a folding ping pong table that has folding ping pong balls. She polishes her furniture so much you can see your face in it. (Now why in heaven's name would I want to do that?!)

She is so anxious to get back to doing housework, when she goes out she wears white rubber gloves. But I have learned that by playing my cards right (and I don't have a stacked deck), I can create the illusion of being a good housekeeper without the drudgery, and have perfected the following plan of attack.

I Was Trampled by a White Elephant

When buying a new house, you can forget about mortgages, location, and foundations. There are really only three things worthwhile remembering.

1. Buy the biggest house you can find so that when your children are grown up and your husband or some other idiot says, "Why don't you get a job and help out with college expenses?" you can say, "With this house?" Don't bring up the fact that 29 of the 32 rooms are permanently closed off.

2. Buy the house far enough away from school so your kids can't come home for lunch.

3. *Always* buy a house with a fireplace, even if you live in the middle of the desert. Dirt can always be blamed on a faulty flue.

Remember, That Dirt Belongs to You

If there is anything as disgusting as a dirty wall, it must be somewhere around my house.

1. I explain away the smudges on my walls as the height marks of my kids which I'm too sentimental to wash off.

2. When wall washing is being discussed, I say, "I haven't been able to do that since the accident." If anyone should ask what accident, prefer not to talk about it.

If my husband had any heart at all, he wouldn't expect me to stay in a house that messy. However, I know my way around and have worked out some useful methods of dealing with housework.

1. Complain about your high water bills. Don't let anyone know they're the minimum.

2. During spring and fall housecleaning time, put your arm in a sling.

3. Drape a rag over the step ladder in front of a window and it will look as if you've been washing.

4. Have an unused dust mop to shake out the front door. Shake the real one out the back door at night.

5. Leave your sink full of dishes. It's a good way to cover up a dirty sink.

Exercise Your Right Not to Exercise

There is only one sure way to get your house cleaned every day—have a party every night. On a morning you just can't get started, phone the doctor to make a house call. In about 40 minutes you'll have everything cleaned up. Then call him back and tell him not to come.

First, the Cellar

1. Hide your husband's golf shoes. He may clean up the cellar looking for them.

2. You can always explain your dirty cellar windows as a civil defense measure until you get sandbags.

Then, Clean Corners

1. Every so often, dig out the corners. It's a good idea even if it does make the middle of the room a mess. I finally did it the other day when I noticed a gopher hole.

On to Pots and Pans

1. To get a roaster clean, send something like baked apples in it to a neighbor. Neighbors always return pans spotless, and you won't have to use a blow torch on it like you usually do.

Windows

1. Keep at least one window pane clean to check the weather. Once when I didn't do this I sent the kids off with umbrellas for six weeks straight.

Dust with Care

1. Don't dust the cupboard shelves. Then you can fit things where they belong on the spots where there's nò dust.

Clean Fixtures

1. Instead of washing the light fixtures, use stronger bulbs. In three years I've gone from 25 watts to a thousand.

A Final Word

1. If your house is so messed up that you must either hire a cleaning lady or a guide, and you decide on a cleaning lady, get one who commutes from out of town so she doesn't talk among your friends.

Where There's Smoke, It's Usually Only Dirt

If somebody – like a husband – tells you to get busy, say, "All right, if you want that bare, clean, sterile look." Often say, "I let my family *live* in our house." Use the words "casual," "comfortable," "informal," a lot. Our house has gone past the "lived in" look. It has more a "no survivors" look.

When a guest can't control himself and finally comments on how terrible your place looks, these replies will help you out.

1. In the summer, blame dust on open windows; in winter, on the furnace.

2. If someone points out a cobweb, quickly say, "Oh, you mean William's science project . . ."

3. You could say, "I would have cleaned but I'm helping my son's pediatrician conduct an allergy test."

What real home is without bugs. Don't worry about bugs on your plants unless you have artificial plants.

1. If you are out someplace and see a cockroach, say something like, "Now what do you suppose that insect is?" Never be able to identify bugs.

2. If worse comes to worst, you can always try to make friends with them.

Dishonesty Is the Best Policy

1. Blame a lot of things – like soiled wall paper, greasy walls, and a dirty basement – on the previous owners, even if you've lived there for 25 years.

2. Get a dog. Dog owners are not expected to have orderly houses. Even if the lazy mutt hasn't moved for years, people will blame all the tossed throw-rugs and beat up furniture on his playfulness. As the owner of an untrained puppy once said, "It takes a heap to make a house a home."

3. A dangerous question from Mrs. Clean, meaning that she'd like to see the upstairs is, "How many bedrooms do you have?" Say, "None." If she asks outright to see the upstairs, tell her they are fake stairs.

4. Mrs. Clean's Mr. Clean will emphasize every point by pounding his fists on the furniture. Lead him to a hard chair instead of a dusty davenport.

5. If summer has passed and you didn't get around to storing the winter clothes, use strong smelling moth spray when you start wearing them again.

6. Remember, sweeping the porch is more effective than sweeping the living room, unless you have a picture window you can be seen through. I have a horrible view out of our picture window. I see myself in the picture window across the street, and you should have heard what I said about that ugly broad before I found out it was me.

7. If your house is really a mess and a stranger comes to the door, greet him with, "Who could have done this? We have no enemies." Or, "You must be from the bomb squad."

Beauty and the Beast

If you've got a face like I have (diary type — a line a day), clean the mirrors often. I don't panic easily, but dusty wrinkles? To get that beauty rest that will keep you as lovely as I am, try the following tricks.

1. If you want to rest and still look busy, sit and fold diapers. I sat and folded diapers for three years after the last kid was trained.

2. When you want to read, sit in front of a book-case with a dust cloth in your hand and books spread all over.

3. Get a decent looking housecoat so you can occasionally pretend the latch slipped behind you and you're locked out, forced to spend eight hours basking in the sun on a chaise longue.

4. Since Mrs. Clean is bound to ring the doorbell just when you're napping, to cover the chenille marks keep a large band-aid handy.

Meet the Presser

1. Never wash on Monday. Why pick a day when you're sure your whites will be compared to somebody else's?

2. Even though your ten-year-old washer still has the Christmas bow it came with intact, talk as if it's been repaired again and again and really needs replacing.

3. If you have already made the mistake of installing a laundry room, here are a few tips that will get you out of it quickly.

   a. Scorch white shirts in front so your husband will insist they be sent to the laundry. Scorch marks on the back aren't a guarantee as he may just leave his jacket on.

   b. Buy your husband a sun lamp. Shirts look whiter on a man with a tan.

4. Vinegar is recommended for almost everything. I have so many dresses with spots removed by vinegar that if I'm not sitting near a salad I worry about the way I smell.

5. Next to baking (pg. 44), sewing is the most domestic thing in the world. The appearance of

being able to sew is better than actually doing it. To create this impression, I recommend:

a. Sprinkling straight pins on the floor.

b. Drawing a black line around several of your daughter's skirts about an inch above the bottom. It will look as if you let down hems.

Keep Your Back to Reality

1. Buy yourself a loving cup that says, "To The World's Best Mom." These are sold in any dime store. People's attitude about your house softens a lot with this staring them in the face.

2. Be careful not to trip on a rug when you have company so they see what's been swept under there. If you do, scream, "Oh, my head!" so their eyes are distracted. However, more efficient housewives do not sweep dirt under rugs—they push it down the cold air ducts.

3. Keep a Good Will bag in your bedroom. It gives the impression all that mess is going to a worthy cause.

4. If your house is a mess don't use the excuse, "I'm in the midst of spring housecleaning" if any of your kids are nearby. One of them is too apt to say, "Mother what's spring housecleaning?"

5. If you misspell a word just say, "I couldn't find it in the dictionary." You don't have to say you couldn't find the dictionary.

6. Have a lot of souvenirs around from far off places, even if you've just sent for them from a mail order house. It will give the impression of your being a world traveler who hasn't been home long enough to have thoroughly cleaned the house.

		Mon.	Tues.	Wed.
MRS. CLEAN'S WEEKLY SCHEDULE	A.M.	Wash	Iron	Light cleaning Clean drawers
	P.M.	Fold and sprinkle clothes	Put clothes away	Wash and set hair

		Mon.	Tues.	Wed.
PHYLLIS' WEAKLY SCHEDULE	A.M.	Send laundry out and go back to bed	Throw returned laundry under bed	Stuff everything in drawers
	P.M.	Nap	Take scheduled makeup nap you missed last week	Beauty parlor

Thurs.	Fri.	Sat.	Sun.
Light cleaning	Cleaning	Bake	Family (Church)
Woman's Club	Brisk walk in fresh air	Grocery shopping	2 hours of concen- trated culture

Thurs.	Fri.	Sat.	Sun.
Rake living room	Shake out dustmop for neigh- bors to see	Call deli- catessen	Forced family time
Beauty parlor	Beauty parlor	Beauty parlor (estimate completed)	Read funnies

What To Say

When A Moth Flies

Out of the Oven

If your oven lights up

So you see what you bake

Remove the bulb

For heaven's sake!

THE MISERY OF EATING

Everytime I go near the stove, the dog howls.

My next house is going to have the kitchen upstairs so I don't keep running into it. I'm such a lousy cook I can't even say to Fang, "If you don't work, you don't eat"—it's no threat. In our house, we have Alka Seltzer *on tap*.

If you cook like I do, the best thing I can tell you is not to be sensitive. Here are some of the insults I've had to overlook: When Fang passes my gravy he says, "One lump or two?" Once I sent a treat to

Boy Scouts and the leader awarded a merit badge to anyone who could eat it. When I entered a cake at the county fair, it was the only one awarded a *black* ribbon. I asked Fang when he choked if he had swallowed wrong. He said, "Well, let's just say with this food it's wrong to swallow."

My coffee is so bad, my guests frequently say, "I'll take cream and sugar, but skip the coffee." Once I said to Fang, "Notice how I captured that flavor." He said, "If I were you, I'd let it loose."

I lay my trouble to getting a late start in cooking. Some women can't boil water when they get married. When I was married I didn't know what water was. All I ever learned at my mother's knee was what a bony knee looked like. But now I can boil water — when I don't forget and use the colander.

These are my tips on being a success in the kitchen without going near the stupid place.

The Casualty List Hasn't Been Released Yet

Planning

1. Don't spend too much time planning meals. You don't want a charge of premeditation.

2. Try to talk people out of eating. Say to your husband, "All right, if you want that sluggish groggy feeling a big breakfast gives you..." When

my family says they've had a hot breakfast, they mean I've served their cornflakes off the radiator.

3. Don't keep apologizing to your husband for your cooking. He could have checked at the high school and found out you got F's in Home Ec.

Serving

1. Never serve meals on time. The starving eat anything.

2. Use small plates and give little servings. It helps your morale if everything is cleaned up. I serve my meals on coasters.

3. If your husband looks at something you've put before him and says, "Oh, good God!" don't ask, "How do you like it?"

4. Food tastes better if you eat outdoors. If possible, picnic 365 days a year.

5. Never picnic with another family where the mother is apt to bring hot chicken and home-made pickles. For years your kids will refer to the picnic where Mrs. So-and-So brought fried chicken.

6. Serve coffee early in the meal and very hot. If a guest burns his tongue he won't be able to taste anything.

7. Add the word supreme to everything you serve —hamburgers supreme, turkey necks supreme, toast supreme, etc.

I Was Booked For Inattentive Cooking

Half of cooking is appearance, and if that's the only half you're capable of, be sure to:

1. Pick up a cook book at a rummage sale so you have one that looks used.

2. Buy an apron, then rip and smudge it.

3. Cook from a little girl's cook book. They use terms like "Brown" and "Cook slow," instead of "Sauté" and "Simmer." Also, it's cheaper to cook with Kool-Ade than with wine.

4. Wear glasses when you're taking something out of the oven. They will steam up and you'll have a few minutes to brace yourself.

5. Do not taste food while you're cooking. You may lose your nerve to serve it.

6. If your cooking is as bad as mine, train your family to eat fast.

7. Above all, use imagination in your cooking. Imagine it's good.

Remember, the disasters that bring families closer together aren't usually the cooking ones.

Expecting the Unexpected

1. If company arrives just at mealtime, smear peanut butter on one of the kid's chins so they'll think you've already eaten.

2. Sometimes the above doesn't work and people actually sit down at the table. Then, if you want to pass a meal off as homemade when you really got everything from the delicatessen, shortly before the guests sit down, have the timer on the stove go off.

3. Discuss religion and politics at a dinner party so people get into heated arguments and don't notice what they're eating. They may also think the arguing caused their indigestion.

4. During the meal, someone is bound to call your food something other than what it is. Don't argue. If they're eating spaghetti and say, "What delicious sauerkraut!" just say "Thank you."

5. One good general rule is, never serve a foreign

dish to people of that nationality. For instance, I found out I don't cook Italian very fluently.

6. If anyone looks as if he is about to get sick, say "Heavens, I forgot to get this recipe over to Evelyn," just as if she had asked for it. They'll think it can't be as bad as they thought it was.

7. Don't be flattered if your guests ask for a doggie bag. They may just want to have the food analyzed.

Marketing Made Easy

1. Spot a domestic looking woman in the super-market and copy her grocery cart.

2. Try to buy packages that do not have pictures of how it's supposed to look. (Once my turkey looked just like the picture in a book, but it tasted like one of the pages.)

3. Don't buy products that advertise that even a child can use them. These failures have a greater sting.

Actually, it doesn't matter what I buy, my food always tastes as if I made it with Brand X. But I do use name brands. Well, what I mean is, every brand I use, Fang calls a name.

Recipes

Later in this book (pg. 52) I have noted some of my most successful recipes. That material has been placed in this book against the advice of my lawyer. He says I could be sued. However, you may wish to remember that when you're out and your husband asks you to get a recipe for something that is served, don't try it for at least a year to make sure he's forgotten what it's supposed to taste like. Of course, after he eats it he will scratch it off the list. Don't bother to recopy it. It probably won't turn out any better the next time.

Now turn to page 52 and bon apetit.

Is It A Pie? Is It A Cake? It's A Casserole!

Nothing gives a greater impression of domesticity than home baked breads. I tried making homemade bread once. It was still on the bird feeder when spring came.

1. At coffee klatches say, "My husband can always tell when I use a mix." Don't tell the whole truth by adding, "He says they taste so much better." When I make anything from scratch, it tastes scratchy.

2. To impress your girl friends, cover empty bread pans with towels and put them in front of a radiator.

3. If you must bake, make pies with out-of-season fruit. Your family will have forgotten what it's supposed to taste like because they haven't eaten any lately.

4. Above all, don't feel you're lying when you use the term home-baked if the bakery is in town.

5. One final invaluable tip: Make a scrapbook for your family, cutting out pictures of baked items and writing "This Is A Pie" and "This Is A Coffee Cake" under them. Then they won't embarrass you when they go out by not being able to recognize them.

What Heloise Doesn't Tell You

1. If you get the sugar and flour in the wrong cannisters, do not wait until they are empty at the same time to switch. I tried waiting and it took 17 years.

2. When you see seven boxes of powdered sugar and eight of cream of tartar, all in use, realize that it's time to combine things.

3. Don't waste time trying to combine items in spray cans as the holes are too small.

4. Replace the labels on store-bought pickles with your own, writing a month and year. Be sure to use the month women ordinarily put up pickles. You can easily find a cobweb to drape on the jar so it looks as if it's been in the fruit cellar.

A Perfect Waste of Calories

Don't follow the adage "Feed a cold." I did once and the way I cook it turned into pneumonia. Just stick to the following rules.

1. When a recipe says "Wash fowl," don't use the dishwasher.

2. If your husband says, "I want you to be an old-fashioned housewife, and you can start by dressing a chicken for Sunday dinner," you know he has to be kidding. I tried it and it took me three weeks to make the blouse.

3. You may not know it, but scotch tape holds a meat loaf together beautifully. I always use it if I'm out of band-aids or rubber bands. A little ketchup will cover up the flavor. Before I did this, I could never slice a meat loaf—it exploded.

4. Never have a counter top built according to your specifications. Always be able to complain it's either too high or too low.

5. On Halloween, don't give out homemade treats. You're just asking for soaped windows.

6. Sometimes when you're in the beauty parlor, ask if you may clip out a recipe that's in one of their magazines. Have a litter bag in the car you can throw it in.

Applied Appliances

No chapter of kitchen hints would be complete without a word about appliances. The few simple rules below will save you hours of labor.

1. Realize it's time to defrost the refrigerator when you see frost on the outside.

2. When you open the refrigerator door, assume a model's stance. No matter what ugliness you behold inside, it will help you if you make yourself feel like Betty Furness.

3. Every few weeks check the fruit in the refrigerator to see if it's a "coming-in" green or an "on-the-way-out" green. In fact, when my family says they're going to raid the refrigerator, they mean spray it with.

4. Having a dishwasher can be an educational experience. They really do a better job than you do. I thought I had milk glass and found out I had crystal.

CHAPTER III

Phyllis Diller's

Successful Recipes

CHAPTER IV

The Hostess With

The Leastest

With my invitations

I send directions as a guide

But my house is such a mess

They need a map for the inside.

HOUSEKEEPING AT ITS WORST

Anyhow you know they're good sports or they wouldn't have accepted your invitation in the first place.

Try to be gracious, but you have to watch what you say. Once I said, "I love to cook for friends," and someone answered, "If this is the way you cook for friends, I'd hate to see how you cook for enemies." Another time I asked, "Dessert now?" They said, "No, we'll stick it out."

But no matter what is said, it is important for the hostess to be gay and at ease. To help attain this status, the following points should help.

False Impressions

You need never ever feel embarrassed again about how rotten your furniture looks. You can always:

1. Give a sentimental value to any piece that looks beat-up. Say, "We'd get rid of that chair with the springs showing, but I was sitting on it when Ronnie brought home his first report card with a grade above an F." *Never* say, "It's either that or sitting on the floor."

2. No matter how well your guests know you, pretend you've got class. When I point out a piece of furniture I say, "That's a Ben Franklin" in a tone that doesn't give away the fact that that's the store where I bought it.

Dial M for Messy

A little intentional sloppiness can cover up weeks of not cleaning your house. Try:

1. Placing a tipped-over flower pot in view. Any dirt within 50 feet can be blamed on this, and anyone knows this is *Better Homes and Gardens*-type dirt.

2. Or, if you prefer, a few cactus plants sitting around will make the sand on the floor look like part of the decor.

3. Buy an easel and leave it lying in a conspicuous place. Much will be forgiven if people think you are an artist.

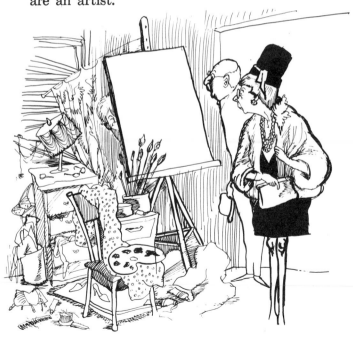

A Few New Wrinkles
(from an expert on wrinkles)

1. Invariably a guest will ask to use the phone, so never have it located in your ever-messy kitchen. Have one put on the front porch.

2. Hook a whisk broom on the bottom of the stair railing so a kid can brush himself off when he comes down.

3. If you do anything new to your house, don't let anyone know. People drop in to inspect.

4. Choose a checked or striped wall paper. People will be halfway home before they are able to focus.

5. Use old newspapers to line your dresser drawers. I tried it and now I have only to look under my husband's handkerchiefs to relive World War II.

6. Convert the downstairs recreation room into a cellar.

The Uninvited

No home should be without these six basic rules for entertaining unexpected guests. Post them on the inside of your refrigerator door.

1. If somebody calls and says they'll be right over, throw everything down the clothes chute, including the kids.

2. Put a chain across the driveway so people don't drive up to the back door and come into the house through your ever-messy kitchen.

3. Explain the way the house looks by saying you're doing a magazine article and can't change anything until you take the "before" pictures. If you have already used this line once, try an

alternate lie: Pretend you're an astrology buff and say, "A Taurus wasn't supposed to start anything today."

4. If a guest is wearing glasses, as he walks out the door grab them before he notices they're clean and say, "Let me wipe the dust off for you."

5. If relatives call and say they are dropping in and you have the horrifying thought that they may want to spend the night, have the family watch TV for six hours straight to develop red eyes, and just before they get there, spray the house with Vicks. If they already have colds, ·you're sunk.

6. If Mrs. Clean catches you in your bathrobe at 11:00 A.M. you have two choices – either grab a bar of soap and drape a bath towel over your arm, or wrap a wool sock around your throat. With the latter, she may even be so sympathetic she'll go home and send you some homemade soup that you can serve the kids for lunch.

Planned Partyhood

1. Only entertain in October. People will be favorably impressed at seeing your storm windows up so early. If they don't live in the neighborhood they won't know they weren't taken down all summer.

2. Always give a hard-times party. They'll think you made the house look that way on purpose.

3. Do not have company when the sunlight is streaming through the windows. Everything shows up. Either entertain at night, or close the drapes and break the cord.

4. No matter what time your guests arrive, pretend they're early, so naturally you're not ready.

What Amy Vanderbilt Doesn't Tell You

1. Have *one* feature that you are well-known for, like big meals, clean kids, or the neighborhood gossip.

2. Volunteer to go around on charity drives. It will make you feel good. You're bound to find somebody in a worse mess than you are. Try to go around collecting at 8:00 in the morning.

3. Tell people you've been developing hobbies to enjoy when the kids are grown. Don't tell them that the hobbies are rocking and napping.

4. Beware of the mother who comes to your house carrying a baby. If she hasn't already seen your bedroom, she may want to lay him on the bed.

5. If company drops in and the children are wearing grimy sweatshirts, have them lie on their stomachs in front of the TV.

6. No matter what anybody drops behind the couch, don't let them retrieve it, whether it's a wrist watch or a diamond ring. Offer to replace it — what's money compared to your ruined reputation?

7. To really impress people, sprinkle alcohol on your kids' underwear. They will think their father is a doctor.

Don't Call Us

In the unlikely event that you are ever invited to a party, remember that:

1. Women of your kind do not wear lapel buttons so they can be recognized, and you can easily find yourself in a group of women who are exchanging recipes or discussing knitting patterns. The only safe way to avoid this is to drift over to a group of men. If they are exchanging recipes or discussing knitting patterns, leave the party. And you'd better take your husband with you.

2. When you go to Mrs. Clean's for dinner and she serves something fancy like lobster thermidor say, "What a coincidence – just what I left for the children."

3. As you're leaving her dinner party say, "I had a lovely time and I'm sure nobody noticed." Then leave quickly.

4. Try to learn a little about flowers. Once when I was out I complimented a hostess on her floral arrangement and she said, "Those are from forsythia," I asked if she lived next door.

CHAPTER V

Remember, My Tranquilizers Are Coming Out of Your Allowance

Are they really so cute
In P.J.'s with Teddies,
Or is it because
They're so near their beddies.

ESSAYS OF A SCREAMING MOTHER

Ah! The magic of childhood! But it doesn't work. I can't make them disappear. I do wear dark glasses in the house hoping they won't recognize me.

To show how wild they are, my eight-year-old bought a bicycle with money he had saved by not smoking. I got one of them a pair of elevator shoes and sent him to school a year early. I had him going to kindergarten and two nursery schools at the same time.

One of my girls was so hard to get along with she was in a Girl Scout troop all by herself. She never smiles. She was 15 before I saw her second teeth, and then I just happened to be with her when they told her she was on Candid Camera.

None of my kids were drop-outs, but they caused several drop-outs among the teachers. They are so hard to live with our next-door neighbors were ready to sell. Well, in fact, they were ready to give.

I signed up for the Foster Parents Plan, but that didn't work. I thought they'd send me some foster parents to help.

And did we have kids! We were sort of an atom bomb in the population explosion. We were having kids so long I went straight from buying Carter's baby clothes to Carter's Little Liver Pills. I was tired out all year signing their names on the

Christmas cards. I finally quit having them by lying to the doctor about my age.

Then Mrs. Clean has the nerve to say things like, "Children grow up too fast." I keep asking mine, "Why can't you be like other kids and grow up too fast?" One day she said, "If they make you so nervous, why did you have so many?" I told her I had them before I knew poodles were going to become so popular. Once she looked at my five and said sweetly, "You're so lucky. How I'd love just one of those." I said, "Frankly, that's what I would have settled for, too."

That not being the case, however, here are some hints on how to live through it from a woman who learned the hard way.

Cleanliness Is Next to Impossible

1. The first rule to remember is, it's the Ivory that floats, not the baby.

2. Don't feel you have to give him a bath every single day. He won't tell anybody.

In Praise of Violence

All children need discipline occasionally. I always say people should raise their kids like they make bread — punch them down after the first rising.

1. Always stick to your guns. I would recommend a Winchester and a Colt .45.

2. Fine your kids a penny for every fight they have. (I did this once and by night time their bicycles had second mortgages.)

3. Don't have your children obey you because they fear you. It's all right to try, but it won't work.

4. Explain to your children they have to behave better. They are making it so difficult for you to complain about other people's children.

5. Make your teenagers show some respect. Try to have them ask for permission before they say, "Are you ever dumb!"

What Dr. Spock Doesn't Tell You

It's a well recognized fact that children are like wild animals, therefore, the most important thing to learn is a few Don'ts. Don't show fear in front of your child – if you fall off, get right back on and ride. Of course, you can always become a den mother so you won't be afraid of your child. Then you'll be afraid of 15 children.

1. Never approach your child with your fingers extended. Make a fist and have a calm, reassuring tone of voice.

2. Don't feel you have to bathe their little bodies every night before they go to bed. In case of fire you can always see to it the firemen spray them first.

3. Don't worry if your kids' faces are always dirty. You may get away with sending them to school while they've got the measles.

Tips from a Planned Parenthood Drop-out

1. As soon as you discover you are pregnant, it's wise to start saving for a rainy day – so you can hire a baby sitter and get out of the house.

2. The baby sitter will be the mainstay of your sanity. Don't feel you should invariably go by child guidance experts, as it isn't always possible to follow their advice. One said, "Always have a baby sitter who is acquainted with your children." If they were acquainted with *my* children, they wouldn't sit!

3. Watch the expression on your baby sitter's face when you refuse to tell her where you can be reached.

He May Be President If You Decide To Let Him Grow Up

1. Don't let your children play with kids whose mothers make homemade cookies. This just gives them false hopes.

2. Teach them not to take a ride from *anyone*. Even if he's harmless, they'll get home too soon.

3. Have fire drills in your home. This was a regular practice at our house until one of the kids thought there should be a real fire.

4. No matter how mad you get at them, do not throw away the instructions on how to give artificial respiration.

5. Try to have your kids play outside as much as possible. Assure them a little lightning won't hurt.

6. If you have adopted children it is kinder to tell them they are adopted. In fact, someone suggested it would be kinder for me to tell my children they're adopted even though they're not.

The Snake Pit Revisited

To live to old age (the time when it's more of a thrill to hear your kids come up the front steps than go down them), I have developed the following suggestions for survival.

1. Hang your kids' pajamas in sight. It keeps your spirits up through the day.

2. If your kids must come home from school for lunch, put ten leaves in the table to keep them apart. Those noon hours are terrible – they feel they have to fight fast.

3. Run the vacuum often. Not to clean – to drown out the kids.

4. Make a rule the only time the kids can run in the house is when they're on their way out. And if they write their names in the dust on the furniture, don't let them put the year.

5. Remember, your sales resistance is lower with a salesman who comes right after the kids have gone to school. When you find out he isn't one of the kids that missed the bus, you're so happy you'll buy anything.

6. Get your kids in the church choir even if they can't sing. What's easier to dress them in on Sunday morning than a choir robe?

7. Tell your kids' teachers you strongly believe the best punishment is having them stay after school.

"Shut Up," Said Mother, "Shut Up, Up, Up."

Traveling with kids is terrible. This is the way we figure mileage — how many miles to a fight. We stopped for a hitchhiker once, he took one look, and refused to get in. I make no guarantees, but maybe the following will help you out.

1. When traveling with kids, it's smart to keep something in your purse to surprise them with —like a blackjack.

2. If you're taking your kids on a vacation, like driving from New York to Disneyland, make a rule that your house has to be out of sight before they start asking, "When will we be there?"

3. Don't point out anything for them to notice as you drive along. You're too apt to be past before they've all spotted it, and I've found it's mighty hard to back up on the expressways.

Every Teenage Girl Needs a Mother To Misunderstand Her

Children learn primarily by observing their parents' behavior so it is wise to set good examples for them to follow. If you sow wild oats your kids will feel they can, too. They'll say, "If you can sow, I can sow, too."

1. Don't drink until the children are in bed. We made this rule once, but they got so sick of getting tucked in at 4:30.

2. Don't pay attention to the rule not to fight in front of your kids. How else is your daughter going to learn how to win an argument?

3. Your daughter should help around the house. This is not easy to accomplish. My girls even fight over who has to press "Start" on the dishwasher.

CHAPTER VI

"You Wouldn't Know
It Was Raining
Outside
Unless the Phone Leaked"

Thank you, Mr. Graham Bell
But would you tell me
What makes my right ear swell?

I may be the only woman in the world who has a tan from the light on her Princess phone. If there were a parking meter in front of that phone, we could have paid off the mortgage. When my husband picks up the phone and it's for me, he says, "Whom shall I say is willing to listen?" So I can give you some good advice on what to say to your husband when he complains about your excessive use of the phone. The following sample conversation may be of some help.

Fang: Can't you ever be off the telephone?

Phyllis: I work all day, and that's the thanks I get. I'm the best housekeeper in the neighborhood!

Fang: What makes you think you're a good housekeeper, just because there isn't any dust on the telephone?

Phyllis: I never get to talk. Did you notice this morning that the minute I got on the phone the kids wanted something?

Fang: Yeah. Breakfast! It was 7:00.

Phyllis: I don't talk on the phone much.

Fang: You don't talk on the phone much! I called ten times today and the line was busy.

Phyllis: I was ordering groceries.

Fang: What do you do? Run a supermarket?

Phyllis: And I had 50 calls to make for the PTA.

Fang: PTA must stand for Public Telephoning Association. Just one day I'd like to have a busy wife instead of a busy line.

Phyllis: You seem to have forgotten the prize I got for making the 50,000th dial phone call.

Fang: Yeah. That was a lot of calls for one person to make in a week. And those dopes you talk to ... Minerva Ratzwrinkle ...

Phyllis: I don't talk to her anymore. Since she got her marriage straightened out, she's a perfect bore. And besides, I'm not interested in gossip.

Fang: I've heard you talk for half an hour to the courtesy time lady.

Phyllis: For your information, last night I hung up 15 minutes after you stepped inside the door.

Fang: Yeah, but you were talking to a wrong number.

Phyllis: I don't have to sit here and take your insults.

And then I hung up on him.

Advice for the Phonelorn

One day I received a phone call from a lady who said, "My husband says I can't be a good mother because I'm always on the telephone. What can I tell him?" I told her to tell him that in the winter the kids can always come in and warm their hands on the phone.

Another woman wrote to me and said, "Dear Phyllis, I tried to call you but your line was busy.

What I want to know is what I can say to my husband who complains that I'm on the phone so much the kids run around the house at 10:00 still in their pajamas." (Signed) Busy Mother. I wrote back, "Dear Busy, Don't say anything to him but tell your kids to start sleeping in their clothes."

Watch out for phrases that give away the amount of time you spend on the phone.

1. Don't start every conversation with "What hath God wrought?"

2. Don't end every conversation with "Bulletins at any second!"

Get a cord that stretches so that you can even empty the garbage can—in the back yard.

CHAPTER VII

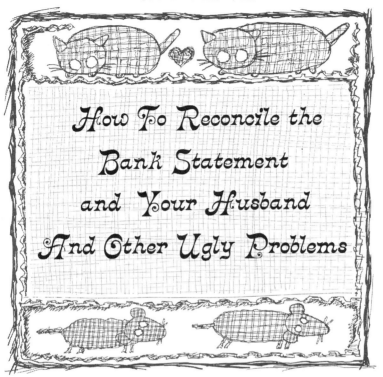

How To Reconcile the Bank Statement and Your Husband And Other Ugly Problems

I want my kitchen remodeled
Before I'm any older.
"I'll do it," said Fang
And got me a new potholder
MISER METHODS

No book on household hints would be complete without a word on the nauseating subject of budgeting so to collect the most expert tips I could, I observed the master miser, Fang.

I know you have to watch where your money goes, but Fang was once hit in the eye by a cash register key.

When he proposed, I thought he had money because he said he spent hours every week clipping coupons. He meant the kind that gives 8¢ off a box of detergent. The wedding ring he bought me was so cheap I just have to look at it to know I'm not happily married.

When we were finally married he moved me into a house so rundown that once when I left a box of clothing on the front porch for the Good Will charity they took the house, too. For the first six months we lived on refunds from double-your-money back guarantees.

Despite the fact that he doesn't make much, I feel he is a little too thrifty. What other family uses a Bible from the library?

Even if the following ideas for saving money are not possible for you to use, at least it will make your husband seem like a philanthropist.

Easy Come, Easy Go

When you're in as rotten a financial condition as we are, it's important to be able to put off your creditors. The following little tricks may be of some help.

1. When you get a letter from a creditor who tries to be polite and says, "It's so easy to forget a little bill like this," write back and say, "Okay, forget it."

2. Of course, everybody knows that charity begins at home. We have perfected that concept. On everybody else's window it says "We Gave." On ours it says, "We'll Take."

May I Stretch Your Budget, Lady?

Most men you go out with realize money talks. Fang doesn't let money even whisper. Nothing slows down his money saving approach.

1. Recently, he started worrying about the cost of our daughter's wedding, so he bought an aluminum ladder that he said *anybody* could lift.

2. When we go out and he buys me a corsage, I know enough not to get him a boutonniere because it would be bigger.

3. When we have guests he puts a cherry in a glass of beer and calls it a Manhattan.

4. We already have pay TV. When our company watches television, Fang passes the hat.

Discount Stores Don't Have Discount Parking Meters

The family car is one of the "expense centers" of any household. My husband said he was buying me an economy car. It didn't have a motor. He says I can't get another one until they invent a car that will run by the rays of the sun. Here are some money saving devices he's figured out.

1. Fang didn't get a heater for the car because he insisted we could heat it with the cigarette lighter.

2. Even on the road you can still save money. When the man in the parkway toll booth hands him a ticket, Fang says, "No, thank you."

3. He insists on fixing the car himself, even though he is so far from mechanical that I've seen him try to look at the engine through the ignition keyhole.

4. The only time we have safety belts is when the chains aren't needed on the tires.

You Don't Get Trading Stamps
When You Go to the Obstetrician

1. At a social gathering, ask any doctor for advice. We were at a party once and Fang said to a doctor, "What should I do about this cough?" The doctor said, "Put your hand over your mouth."

2. For Christmas, give each of the kids a gift certificate to the dentist. Fang is so afraid of going to the dentist himself that he once went disguised as a pregnant woman.

3. Stay drunk. Fang can't bear to spend money on glasses because he knows he always drinks so much that they wouldn't help anyhow.

House of Horrors

Fang hates to call a serviceman. The other day he called the plumber and asked if he could bring the leak in and have it fixed. He has devised some ingenious methods of fixing things.

1. The roof leaked over our bedroom. When I told him to take care of it, he bought me a pair of all-weather pajamas.

We're always running out of fuel oil because Fang buys it by the quart. If I ever turn the heat on when the temperature is above 30, he accuses me of arson. He has discovered some methods that seem to hold promise for saving on the heating bills.

1. Last winter we were heating with liniment.
2. We turn down the heat while the candles on a birthday cake are lit.

New Tricks from an Old Dog

Fang will never be accused of being the last of the big spenders. He wants to be so sure he gets his money's worth that once he went to a stag dinner where a burlesque queen jumped out of a cake, and he asked, "*Now* what are we going to have for dessert?"

The last time he took me out for a drink was when our town gave Sabin liquid vaccine free. I finally tricked him into taking me out to eat by telling him it would cut down on the grocery bill. It had been so long since the last time that when the waiter asked me what I wanted, I said, "A pound of sirloin." And the cheap restaurant he took me to! It was so bad that the Humane Society stopped them from giving out doggie bags.

Here's Fang's favorite restaurant money saver: Instead of tipping, he shakes hands.

Home on $5 a Day

Nobody knows how to save money on vacation as well as Fang. When we were going together he promised every year he'd take me to the seashore.

The nearest I got to the seashore was a Hamilton Beach vacuum cleaner. Some of his most recent tricks are:

1. Last year he bought me the book *Hawaii* and gave me some seasick pills.

2. Asking for economy class tickets when we take the subway.

3. Of course, he has suffered some reverses. He found out you can't get your phone disconnected every time you're going out of town for the weekend, but he tried.

He's an Emotional Spender—Cries While He's Shopping

1. Once when I was out of town I asked Fang to wire me some flowers. He put two rose petals inside a 35¢ telegram.

2. Instead of getting me a new Easter outfit, every year Fang takes me to a different church. The year after we made the Hindu Temple, we moved out of town.

3. Instead of eggs on Easter, our kids color pumpkin seeds he's had them save from Halloween.

4. He buys such cheap appliances that instead of a warranty we get a warning.

5. He buys that hair cream that advertises "a little dab'll do ya," and he only uses half a dab.

6. Last year Fang not only made his own Christmas cards, he made his own stamps.

My Husband Caught Me in the
Arms of Morpheus

From the moment you and your husband get up in the morning, be alert. Your first problem will be to get back into bed. This can be solved in several ways.

1. Pretend you're economizing. Ask him if he wanted you to waste the heat still left in the electric blanket.

2. Be sure to have a bottle of sleeping pills in the medicine chest. If your husband thinks you have trouble sleeping, he might not believe you nap as often as you do.

This may not be necessary for you to get your husband up, but with Fang I use a plunger.

The Return of the Wolfman

Supposing you're a housewife and you've goofed. Let's put it this way, it's 4:30 and you're still in bed—and that's pretty close to "Ogre Time"—try the following:

1. Put a little O'Cedar way behind each ear; it makes you smell tired.

2. Splash cold water on your face. If you pant a little, it looks exactly like beads of sweat.

3. Rouge your knees. It will look like you have been scrubbing the floors.

4. Have a broken strap hanging from your sleeve. It gives the impression you've been reaching and stretching.

5. Let your husband see you take off your shoes and rub the bottoms of your feet.

What Dr. Brothers Doesn't Tell You

1. Make a list of things to do. Check them off and leave the list where your husband can see it. Only one man in 10,000 will check to see whether or not they're done.

2. Never go out in the middle of the week without yawning all evening.

3. To avoid having your husband complain you're giving him for dinner the same thing he's had for lunch, louse it up so he won't know if it's the same thing or not.

4. If you are single, get married on Thanksgiving Day so you can insist upon eating out on your anniversary.

5. If your husband's on a damn special diet, like three meals a day, use all the shortcuts you can find. I even buy frozen toast.

6. Have your husband call home at noon. He'll find it's easier to take half-a-day's complaints at a time.

7. When your husband wants to go out with the boys, let him. It's easier to sulk than to be nice to him.

Never Go to Bed Mad—Stay Up and Fight

Just the other day I said to Fang, "Don't you think we've got a storybook romance?" and he said, "Yes, and every page is ripped." I recommend:

1. Periodically renewing your vows—not the vows that you'll kill him if he's late for dinner or forgets your anniversary—your marriage vows.

2. Using terms of endearment when you fight, like, "Sweetheart, you know I can't stand your fathead mother, darling," and "Sweetie, I'm leaving you, honey, if you ever drink that much again."

3. Do romantic things, like scrubbing the kitchen floor by candlelight.

CHAPTER VIII

Where There's A Will

There's A Way Out

Unhand me housework
You're no thriller
I'd rather be gorgeous
Like Phyllis Diller.
PHYLLISOPHICAL SAYINGS

There are a couple of problems even I haven't been able to solve, like what to say when somebody notices one of the holes in the acoustical ceiling is moving, or what to say when a piece of tinsel shows from under the rug in May. But I have compiled quite a list of advantages I've discovered in housekeeping the Phyllis Diller way.

1. The paint isn't one bit chipped. The dirt protects it.

2. There are no bugs. The dust has choked them to death.

3. Guests never walk through your glass doors.

4. When I've lost something in our house, I've got at least ten things to look for at the same time.

5. I can tell how much the plumber should charge by knowing he came during the middle commercial of "As the World Turns" and left just before "Password."

6. If I ever become an alcoholic, friends wouldn't suspect I was hiding bottles. They would think it was just my housekeeping. But I'll never become one because I don't like to drink in front of the kids, and when they're not around, who needs it?

7. You don't have to be as careful about knowing where you've put things if you have three of everything.

8. I don't have to change menus for weeks at a time. Every night it turns out different.

9. If I didn't cook the way I did, Fang would never have been able to buy enough food for our five kids. They've yet to ask for seconds and they never complain about the school lunch program.

10. My cooking also makes it easy for kids to learn to share.

11. It also makes dieting a pleasure. People have been known to start diets at my house on Thanksgiving Day.

12. Fang will never get into an accident hurrying home to my meals.

13. You'll be a better conversationalist trying to keep your guests interested so their eyes don't wander.

14. Kids get plenty of physical fitness exercise at school by their trips to the principal's office.

15. The telephone needn't be a horrible expense. I picked up some good money selling spot announcements to local merchants.

16. There are even some advantages to having a stingy husband. For instance, he wouldn't think of playing a slot machine. And if he ever drops a bundle at the race track, it will only be his lunch. He's cheap with himself, too. He made himself a sun dial wrist watch. When anybody asks him what time it is, he has to run outdoors.

17. I've never had to worry about doing anything new to our house. Some men are status seekers. Fang's a status quo seeker.

18. I don't have anything to give up for Lent.

The main advantage for you of following the suggestions in this book is to give you more time to
beautify yourself and you may some day look like
me.

CHAPTER IX

The Diller

Housekeeper's Fest

The Diller Housekeeper's Test

1. Q. If your kids are driving you crazy, should you take a drink or a tranquilizer?

   A. Tranquilizer. Remember, when you get to the PTA meeting nobody is going to say, "Madam, I smell tranquilizers on your breath."

2. Q. Why should you go to PTA meetings: (1) to improve the school system, (2) to get acquainted with the teachers, (3) to meet parents of your kids' friends, (4) all of the above?

   A. None of the above. The reason for going to PTA meetings is that with any luck you may get them to lengthen the school day.

3. Q. What do you do if you are too lazy to clean under the bed?

   A. Use bedspreads that touch the floor. There was a time I didn't do this and one day a guest said to me, "Imagine! Dust ruffles made of dust!"

4. Q. If a neighbor gives you an eggplant from his garden, what can you make of it?

   A. A centerpiece. I once had an artistic display of 250 cucumbers on my dining room table.

5. Q. What can you do with leftover sauerkraut?

A. In December you can silver it and hang it on the Christmas tree. It stinks, but it's pretty. Any other time of year your're on your own.

6. Q. What aspect of housekeeping the Diller Way is illustrated by the picture below?

Please study this picture carefully before attempting to answer the question.

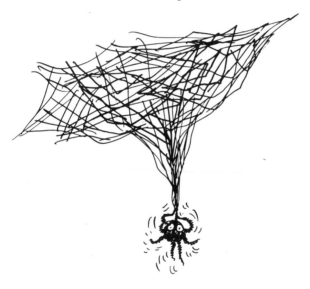

A. After the party, never start to clean up if some of your guests are still hanging around.

7. Q. What aspect of housekeeping the Diller Way is illustrated by the picture below?

Please study this picture carefully before attempting to answer the question.

A. Always keep extra food in the house because you never know who'll drop in.

8. Q. How can you tell when your husband's shirts need replacing?

A. When you can't tell where the iron stops and the shirt starts, they're too gray.

9. Q. How can you avoid jobs like painting the kitchen?

   A. The best attack is the phrase, "Well, if you don't consider my time worth more than . . ." Only one husband in a thousand will have the nerve to say anything.

10. Q. When things are really bad, what's the best explanation?

    A. Never try to explain the mess. Just buy a couple of get-well cards and place them on the mantle. People will assume you've been sick and unable to clean.

11. Q. How can you decide on the best location in which to buy a house?

    A. For women of our type there are several good rules of thumb: (1) Never buy in a neighborhood where the upstairs windows are shining. (2) Avoid neighborhoods where you see wash on the lines at 7:00 Monday morning. (3) A vicinity in which you see a woman hanging laundry after dark will probably be acceptable.

12. Q. What do you do with two years of unironed laundry?

    A. If your family hasn't missed what's in the bag for that long, throw it out.

13. Q. If someone phones and hints for an invitation to come over, what can you do?

A. Feign a cold. Blow into a corner by the phone. The dust will produce coughing, and perhaps even a sneeze.

14. Q. If it's almost time for your husband to come home and you've spent the day eating candy and reading the latest Harold Robbins novel, what do you do?

A. Tie yourself to a kitchen chair and tell him you were playing cowboy and Indians with the kids.

15. Q. Are hand-me-downs psychologically harmful to a second child in the family?

   A. Yes. Try to get some new things for him. We went all out with new things for our first child and the second one had nothing but hand-me-downs. The bronzed baby shoes almost killed him.

16. Q. What's the best way to decorate your home?

   A. Choose a period as obscure as possible so people won't know if it's authentic or not. I particularly recommend the William Jennings Bryan era.

PLEASE TURN OVER FOR

THE DILLER HOUSEKEEPER'S

TEST SCORE CARD

SCORE YOURSELF ON TH

	RIGHT	1/2 RIGHT
1.		
2.		
3.		
4.		
5.		
6.		
7.		
8.		
9.		
10.		
11.		
12.		
13.		
14.		
15.		
16.		

Add _____

DILLER HOUSEKEEPER'S TEST

1/4 RIGHT	1/64 RIGHT

SCORE

1–4·3/64 right   Reread book

4·1/16–9 right   Average slob

9·1/64–15·63/64 right   Better-than-average slob

16 right   You cheated ... now you're learning

Total

DILLER'S DO-IT-YOURSELF INDEX

DILLER'S DO-IT-YOURSELF INDEX *Continued*

DILLER'S DO-IT-YOURSELF INDEX *Concluded*